Living Together

Why Marriage Is the Best Choice

Ellen Dykas

New Growth Press
WWW.NEWGROWTHPRESS.COM

New Growth Press, Greensboro, NC 27404
www.newgrowthpress.com
Copyright © 2016 by Harvest USA

All rights reserved. No part of this publication may be reproduced, stored in a retrieval system, or transmitted in any form by any means, electronic, mechanical, photocopy, recording, or otherwise, without the prior permission of the publisher, except as provided by USA copyright law.

Unless otherwise indicated, all Scripture quotations are taken from the *Holy Bible, English Standard Version*®. Copyright © 2000; 2001 by Crossway Bibles, a division of Good News Publishers. Used by permission. All rights reserved.

Scripture quotations marked NIV are taken from THE HOLY BIBLE, NEW INTERNATIONAL VERSION®, NIV® Copyright © 1973, 1978, 1984, 2011 by Biblica, Inc.® Used by permission. All rights reserved worldwide.

Cover Design: Tandem Creative, Tom Temple,
tandemcreative.net
Typesetting: Lisa Parnell, lparnell.com

ISBN: 978-1-942572-43-5 (Print)
ISBN: 978-1-942572-44-2 (eBook)

Library of Congress Cataloging-in-Publication Data
    Names: Dykas, Ellen, 1965– author.
    Title: Living together : why marriage is the best choice / Ellen Dykas.
    Description: Greensboro, NC : New Growth Press, 2016.
    Identifiers: LCCN 2015042167 | ISBN 9781942572435 (print) | ISBN 9781942572442 (ebook)
    Subjects: LCSH: Unmarried couples—Religious aspects—Christianity. | Marriage—Religious aspects—Christianity.
    Classification: LCC BT705.9 .D95 2016 | DDC 248.8/44—dc23
    LC record available at http://lccn.loc.gov/2015042167

Printed in China

23 22 21 20 19 18 17 16   1 2 3 4 5

Lauren and Will were inseparable almost from the moment they met their junior year in college. Their love for people and Bible study drew them together at the weekly meeting of their Christian fellowship group for college students. They began to date and both wondered if marriage was in the future for them.

The possibility was both exciting and scary. Will hadn't dated seriously before Lauren, but he knew that she was "the one." Lauren sincerely loved Will, but she had already had two serious relationships prior to him and both involved sex. Now she and Will were sexually intimate too. Their love was passionate and exciting, yet both felt insecure about making a lifelong commitment. They decided to save money post-graduation and to test their exclusivity by living together in his townhouse. He didn't want another guy roommate and it would give Lauren the "test step" she needed to discover whether she and Will could be married.

Elizabeth and Rob felt they had the dream relationship. They met, fell in love quickly, and had similar life goals: career success, involvement in community and church, and the joy of sharing life with a compatible person. They were familiar with messy relationships because Rob's first marriage ended after his affair and Elizabeth's marriage dissolved when her husband's verbal abuse escalated to physical violence. Rob and Elizabeth had experienced significant healing and transformation in the years leading up to their first date and both sensed that they'd found someone with whom they could share life in a wonderful and fulfilling way. They considered themselves "married" before God and each other and didn't see the need for the legal or formal setting of a marriage license or church ceremony. Sharing life, sharing a house, sharing bills . . . it all seemed just right (and safe).

John's wife of thirty years died after a long battle with cancer, and he managed on his own quite well for the next several years. But as he began to feel the need for extra help with some of the daily realities of life, he decided to move into a transitional retirement community. His two-bedroom apartment was ideal since his adult kids and grandkids could visit easily. He was lonely, however, and at times felt anxious about his savings carrying him through for as many years as he would need.

When he met Carol, a fun-loving widow, they easily connected and a warm friendship began to grow that eventually turned into a romantic relationship. Both John and Carol felt that at this stage in their lives, there was no need to go through all the formality of getting married. Both felt that to marry each other would somehow betray the memory of their first spouse. And, when Carol confided in John that she too had fears about finances, the decision to move in together seemed like a no-brainer.

* * *

These three examples are common, and cohabitation in the United States is a growing and popular option. Perhaps you're reading this minibook because you've already chosen to live with someone or are considering it for the near future. In the past 50 years, those choosing to live together without being married have increased by more than 1,500 percent. In 1960, about 450,000 unmarried couples lived together. As of a few years ago, the number had grown to more than 7.5 million. The majority of young adults in their twenties will live with a romantic partner at least once, and more than half of all marriages will be preceded by cohabitation.[1]

There are lots of reasons people choose to live together, as the three stories above illustrate. Many churched couples make a persuasive case for why this is not only a wise, but a God-honoring decision. If two consenting adults want to "wisely" discern if someone is a compatible marriage partner, and if finances can be stewarded more frugally, and if there is an inner heart commitment already, what's really the big deal anyway?

God's Perspective on Romantic Relationships

God's original intent was that men and women would enjoy rich community and relationships. He created marriage as a unique relationship between a man and a woman, not only as a blessing for them and for society, but as a way to point to him and his love for his people. This happens as a man and a woman join together in a lifelong, committed relationship with God at the center of their lives.

While God also gives singles the offer of deep relationships through friendship, marriage is distinct. It is the one relationship in which God grants the blessing of a primary relationship of oneness in all areas, as a new family is formed when two people join in a lifelong, exclusive committed relationship. Marriage is the starting point and the goal of a romantic relationship where two people become deeply intimate on every level—emotionally, financially, physically, and sexually.

Paul wrote in Ephesians 5:21–33 about how husbands and wives should care for each other, but at the end of this long discourse, he makes a startling turn in his argument. He said, "'Therefore a man shall leave his father and mother and hold fast to his wife, and the two shall become one flesh.' This mystery is profound, and I am saying that it refers to Christ and the church" (vv. 31–32). Paul made it clear that marriage was intended to be a signpost that pointed beyond itself to the spiritual reality of God's relationship with his people.

This relationship, based on grace through Jesus Christ, is founded upon God's eternal, exclusive relationship with his people, which is initiated by his loving pursuit and entered into by a person's own faith-fueled response. Christian marriage mirrors this: it is entered into by a man and woman, both consenting adults, who pledge before God and others to be a loving, lifelong, exclusive, no-exit-strategy-planned spouse to each other. This commitment, foundational to God's design, sets the stage for a man and woman to grow into a deeper trust and security as they build a life together.

Adults who choose to bypass God's design for marriage experience so much less than what he had in mind for romantic relationships. If this is true, then what's the draw to bypass marriage and simply move in together?

Reasons People Choose to Live Together

There are probably as many unique reasons people choose cohabitation as there are cohabiting couples! If you are considering or just beginning such a relationship, do you see yourself giving one of these reasons?

1. *Fear.* Like Lauren and Will, you might be simply afraid of the enormity of a lifelong commitment to someone. Many couples enter into romantic alliances with each other carrying painful baggage from the past. Also, growing up in a culture of easy divorce, you might have seen few positive examples of strong, loving marriages that have gone the distance. Living together then becomes a preventative measure to protect against a messy and anguishing divorce, should you decide that you really are incompatible with the one you currently love.

   Another reason might be that you feel pressure to move in. You might be afraid of being alone—maybe for a long time or for a lifetime—and you might give in to sharing both a residence and a bed in hopes that marriage will be on the horizon. Or you might be afraid that if you don't move in together, the relationship will end.

The experience of painful and broken relationships in the past, and especially the trauma of divorce, erodes trust in the reliability of someone's verbal oath of faithfulness, and trust in the belief that an "official" commitment really makes any difference. Cohabitation seems to provide an easier and less painful alternative if a relationship doesn't work out. Oftentimes, couples slide into living together rather than *deciding* to commit to a long-term relationship; sleeping over at each other's homes becomes more frequent and eventually a shared household comes into place.

Whatever reason you might have, you need to realize that no human strategy can prevent relational pain. That is only an illusion. No relationship is without struggle and pain, and even the prospect of ending. If two people slide out of a relationship that includes cohabiting, it isn't as pain-free or easy as it might seem at first. Lives, belongings, friends, and households have become shared and entwined, and the dissolution *will still feel* like a divorce when the relationship ends.

2. *Test things out.* Connected to fear and insecurity, many see cohabitation as a way to come to as clear a conclusion about the viability of the relationship as possible: *Will this person make a suitable spouse for me?* Have you thought about the following questions as reasons for pursuing a live-in relationship?

- Will this person be a good fit for me emotionally, sexually, and relationally?
- Will I be happy and content living 24/7 with this person?
- Can we live together with love and respect, or will we face conflict all the time?
- How many checks can I put in the column for "get married," and are they more than the checks in the "get out" column?
- And if I find it's not working out, won't it be easier and simpler to break up?

Wisdom before engagement absolutely necessitates that a couple have discernment regarding strengths and weaknesses, whether they have a similar vision for life and service, and a common commitment to God and unity regarding a lifestyle of worship and obedient love before him. However, you can't "practice" the lifelong nature of marriage through a short-term experience. When you use cohabitation to test the waters, you need to face a blunt assessment—you are operating from a focus on self. *Will this work out for me? If, after a while, I can say yes, I can make a commitment; if no, I'll just step away and **out**.*

Self-focus, and a pursuit of "what's in it for me" is the reason most relationships fail! The relationship becomes a performance evaluation, and both of you are under each other's critical gaze. This is *not* the way God enters into relationship with his people! The kind of relationship you are considering needs a stronger foundation. When two people entwine their lives together while keeping a back door open, they actually increase the odds of walking through that door when times get tough. And all relationships get tough at some point.

And, in addition, when you give only part of your life to someone while at the same time refusing to totally commit, you are not truly loving another. You are loving yourself because your bottom line is your own self-protection.

3. *Financial stress.* John and Carol's awareness of limited finances made merging their households seem like a win-win situation. Their scenario may become an option that older singles will increasingly consider. But even younger singles experience financial stresses. An up-and-down economy and a constant struggle of not having enough money can become another reason to live together, and a financially savvy one too.

Sharing expenses and making your present living situation less stressful is a very shaky foundation. What will you do if your partner loses his or her income through unemployment or physical or emotional injury, and you are still in testing mode in your relationship? The notion of "what's in it for me" will become sorely tested as you begin to shoulder more responsibility to keep financially afloat. Money has never been a glue to keep people together; it is more likely to tear your relationship apart.

4. *Marriage is an unnecessary formality.* Like Elizabeth and Rob, many singles begin living together in a spousal-type relationship, without the formal commitment of marriage, because they feel they are "married in their hearts." This might be where you are right now. Couples like this might defend their situation by saying that they *do* feel like they have a lifelong commitment to one another and are not merely testing things out. In their minds, the formality (and sometimes the perceived hassle and unnecessary cost) of a ceremony and marriage license seem to be burdensome add-ons to the love and faithfulness they have already pledged to one another.

But what one feels and what one actually promises are two different things. Relationships that are based on a public commitment before family and friends have an inherent strength, and they contain a much greater likelihood of both giving and receiving the kind of love the other wants.

Marriage Vows: Why Public Promises Are Significant

So if the reasons for living together don't hold water, biblically and practically, what's the big deal for having a ceremony and getting married? It's just a human tradition, right?

Well, yes and no. While there is no explicit command in the Bible for a public ceremony, there is *biblical understanding* that a marriage begins with a public commitment before a couple's community. God calls a man and a woman into a lifelong relationship with a commitment that is a public, holy promise.

1. Public

God's people have always understood that marriage, which is expressed in Scripture as "one flesh," (see Genesis 2:24; Matthew 19:5) involves a total commitment that is publicly demonstrated. Jesus affirmed the public nature of marriage in his reference to the account of Adam and Eve in Genesis, where their total commitment to each other was a public demonstration of beginning a new family by separating from one's family of origin. This argues strongly against the personal and/or private moving-in arrangement, even when it feels like it's a marriage in spirit. Establishing a separate family unit, with all the life-long implications connected to that, involves one's community. Marriage creates a new family, and the community of God's people—who are witnesses to the marriage—have the responsibility to assist the couple to grow into their public vows.[2]

2. A Holy Promise of the Deepest Kind

Marriage is not merely a cultural institution by which people merge lives, bank accounts, and homes. While the public ceremony has different shapes in different cultures, Jesus said in Mark 10:6–9 that marriage is significant. John Piper comments,

> From the beginning of creation, "God made them male and female" [Genesis 1:27],

"Therefore a man shall leave his father and mother and hold fast to his wife, and the two shall become one flesh" [Genesis 2:24]. So they are no longer two but one flesh. What therefore "*God has joined together*, let not man separate." This is the clearest statement in the Bible that marriage is not a merely human doing. The words "God has joined together" means it is *God's* doing.[3]

Christian marriage is a sign that points to God's relationship with us. Look at just a few of the passages in the Bible where God describes his relationship to his people like a marriage: Isaiah 54:5; Jeremiah 31:31–32; Hosea 2:16; Revelation 21:2. Do you see? God joins a man and woman together in a covenant of marriage, a unique and lifelong commitment based on a promise of grace and selfless love. The marriage covenant gives us a picture of the covenant of grace in which God has entered into an eternal relationship with his people, demonstrated most vividly through the death and resurrection of Jesus Christ.

Marriage Requires Hard Work, but It's Worth It!

To be a faithful spouse in a God-honoring marriage is more than difficult: it's impossible without the love and power of Jesus Christ! Even more than the blessing of companionship, the pleasure of sexual love, the bearing and raising of children, and having a lifelong primary relationship in which to experience trust and safety, marriage's divine meaning is to point beyond itself. A man and a woman, living in a covenant of marriage, have a unique calling to be a signpost to the eternal reality of God's relationship with his people.

As sinful people live in the sweetness and sanctification of a 24/7 relationship with no easily available escape ramps, such things as selfishness, personal agendas, and stubborn individualism are exposed on a daily basis. The process of working through such challenges is actually one of the means through which God transforms a couple in view of such Scriptures as Romans 8:28–29. "And we know that for those who love God all things work together for good, for those who are called according to his purpose. For those whom he foreknew he also predestined to be conformed to the image of his Son, in order that he might be the firstborn among many brothers."

God uses marriage for the good of conforming men and women into the image of Jesus, and the lifelong commitment protects both spouses from running away when this process is painful. Trust, honesty, interdependence, and a shared dependency upon God knit a couple together over time as they move forward through life as one flesh, joined together before God.

Because marriage is hard work, discerning if you should marry someone, even if you have lived together, is a process that is vital to walk through. Often Christians who have chosen to live with a romantic partner outside of marriage have pushed

Jesus aside for the sake of this relationship. Christian marriage calls those considering it to reflect on an eternal truth: that there is someone we are called to love more than a husband or wife. Jesus said, "If anyone comes to me and does not hate his father and mother, his wife and children, his brothers and sisters—yes, even his own life—he cannot be my disciple" (Luke 14:26 NIV). Jesus's extreme words are meant to get across a crucial point for the believer—if you would love someone else, love God first and foremost. Rightly so, because God will not accept second place in your life.

Marriage is a beautiful gift from God, but it is not the ultimate gift—God is! One of the most challenging but worthwhile aspects for you to consider regarding marrying your romantic partner is that God must be central to this relationship. Are you willing to allow him to be the loving Lord over this relationship and to allow your heart to be captivated with him more than the benefits you receive from the other person?

A difficult to grasp biblical truth is that in order to gain true life, we must lose the hold we have on our personal agendas. Instead of choosing to love a partner, spouse, or idea of a spouse, more than anything else—which results in disappointment, pain, and disillusionment—we surrender all to Jesus by faith, and trust that he knows what he is doing. In return we gain our life back in him and experience the joy of walking in obedience. When it comes to romantic relationships, including marriage, God's plan is that as a couple chooses to love Jesus more than anything else, a Christ-centered love will grow between them. Then spouses love each other out of an inexhaustible well of God's love for them.

Marriage *is* hard work, but it *is* worth it, as a rich life of love for God and others will grow as you abandon your dreams and agendas for relationships that don't line up with his!

What Will It Look Like to Step onto God's Path Now?

If you're living with someone outside of marriage, God's kindness, love, and commands are meant to lead you back onto his path (see Romans 2:4). David, a man who walked closely with God and sinned deeply against him, cried out in the Psalms, "I will offer to you the sacrifice of thanksgiving and call on the name of the LORD. I will pay my vows to the LORD in the presence of all his people" (Psalm 116:17–18).

Our devotion to God is humbly lived out in the presence of others, and your steps of obedience will involve both personal choices and public obedience. Consider the following suggestions as ways to begin honoring and obeying God's unique design for relationships. These involve some difficult decisions, but ones that intentionally seek his blessings.

Love God from your heart through obedience

Repentance, which is turning away from sin and back to the direction of God's ways, is rooted in a changed heart posture toward our behavior and choices. "Repentance is turning away from sin (self-reliance) and resolving by God's strength to forsake it, even as we turn to him in faith. Genuine repentance is more fundamentally a matter of the heart's attitude toward sin than it is about change of behavior. Do we hate sin and war against it, or do we cherish it and defend it?"[4]

God is calling you, as an unmarried person, to humbly change your heart's attitude toward your living situation. In faith—and enabled by God's Spirit—your path now needs to focus on taking steps to want Christ and his design for relationships more than you want your current living situation. This kind of love for Christ begins when we become aware of any sin and go to him for forgiveness. The apostle John wrote, "My little children, I am writing these things to you so that you may not sin. But if anyone does sin, we have an advocate with the Father, Jesus Christ the righteous" (1 John 2:1).

God delights to pour compassion over those who are willing to renounce living outside the boundaries of his word (Proverbs 28:13). And he lovingly desires to restore what sin seeks to destroy (Joel 2:25–27). He does not, however, smile or wink upon ongoing disobedience and abuse of his grace when we cherish sin. Your first step, then, is to ask God for a heart change, which he will give you if you go to him.

God is holy, and yet he is also a sympathetic Helper and High Priest. Jesus lived his earthly life as a holy and faithful man in all areas of life, including relationships and sexuality as an unmarried person. He is not a distant God sitting on a throne with no idea of what this feels like for you. Consider how the writer of Hebrews expressed this.

> Since then we have a great high priest who has passed through the heavens, Jesus, the Son of God, let us hold fast our confession. For we do not have a high priest who is unable to sympathize with our weaknesses, but one who in every respect has been tempted as we are, yet without sin. Let us then with confidence draw near to the throne of grace, that we may receive mercy and find grace to help in time of need. (Hebrews 4:14–16)

Jesus is sympathetic to the fears, loneliness, temptations, and struggles you may face as you honor him with your life and this decision. And even more, he has mercy and help to give for your every need.

Surrender the gifts of marriage that you have been sharing

Your trust in Jesus will express itself in your situation as you and your partner take the necessary steps to live as godly singles. This means that both of you commit to sexual faithfulness, which is expressed through abstinence for anyone outside of marriage. This will be difficult (probably very much so), as this has become a regular aspect of expressing care for one another. However, God's Spirit gives us everything we need to walk in obedience as painful as it may be (2 Peter 1:3–4).

You may not realize that your sexual relationship is actually blurring your discernment of whether your relationship is healthy and can last. Why? Because sex is designed by God to *bind* two people together. This powerful binding effect is only safely found in a marriage of commitment; it becomes a connecting power that blesses both spouses. So if you are using sex to test the relationship, you are going about it in a self-focused way that will actually weaken the relationship. This step of honoring God—moving away from your sexual relationship—is what will help you see the relationship more clearly and cultivate ways of relating that will develop deeper trust in one another.

Another action step of obedience will be for one of you to move out of your shared space as soon as possible. Not only is this a practical step to safeguard against sexual temptation, but it is a way to demonstrate love for God and your partner. God's Word defines love differently from the way the world shapes it based on our emotions. Obedience to Jesus always leads us to love others selflessly, pursuing what is good for them according to God's ways (1 John 5:2). And, as we walk in his ways, we grow in other ways that are foundational to healthy, long-lasting relationships: *spiritual and emotional maturity and growth in serving, trusting one another, and pointing one another toward Christ.*

If you've lived together for any length of time, your lives and households may have become fused into one. The dissolving of this situation will most likely require a lot of time and emotional energy, but it is necessary to work through these complexities. If one of you owns the home—or is the primary renter—in which the two of you have been living, then it is most likely right and wise for the non-owner to trust God to provide another living situation. But there can be more difficult complications.

If you have children in this relationship, then considering their needs will be of primary importance. Situations like these may make this path of obedience seem overwhelming, but take each step in wisdom and trust God for the outcome. He takes great delight in costly obedience and will oversee the details of the process in front of you.

Take each step of faithfulness with others to help you. Don't try to go it alone or with only your partner's support. Good friends, wise and seasoned pastors, and church leaders should be with you as you move forward. Allow them to give their input, and together with them pray for the wisdom God gives those who seek his will. God doesn't want us to make these hard decisions entirely on our own. It is his design to provide friends who will both comfort us and challenge us when obedience is painful and costly. Taking the steps to dissolve your household, abstain from sexual activity, and to surrender the marriage-like dynamics that perhaps you've grown accustomed to will be challenging. As our Father who is full of compassion for us, his children, God promises to comfort us (2 Corinthians 1:3–4).

If you realize that you don't have wise and spiritually mature friends in your life to whom you can turn, pray! Ask God to lead you to wise friends who love God and will walk with you. Second, seek the counsel and prayers of a respected pastor, spiritual leader, or mature believer in your life. These are people God calls to bring biblical wisdom to those in need. You will need all the help you can get.

It's possible that you may face another painful consequence of your obedience to not live together anymore: your partner may oppose your decision and threaten to leave the relationship if you move out. This would actually serve to indicate that your relationship has aspects of immaturity and unhealthiness, not to mention selfishness on the part of your partner. In such situations, you can be assured of the wisdom and health of your decision to obey God.

Actually, as anguishing as this might be, it would also be an invitation for you to participate in the sufferings of Christ, himself a man despised and forsaken by the ones he had shared his life with most closely. Are you willing to follow Christ, trusting in him with all your heart even if it ushers you into the intimate place of sharing in his suffering? Will you trust his promise to never leave you and to lead you in the way you should go (see Psalms 32:8; 86:11; Proverbs 3:5–7)?

Cultivate your relationship with your partner according to God's Word

If both you and your partner are willing and committed to go forward in this new path, you now have the opportunity to grow into the best of what God intends for spouses to be. In his design, we are to relate to one another within the gracious boundaries of wisdom as revealed in his Word.

How can you both seek Christ as you relate to one another with trust, respect, sacrificial love, and kindness? Without being sexual, you can focus your energies on developing deeper spiritual and emotional intimacy with one another. It may seem counterintuitive to what you feel as you read these words, but stepping *away from* living together actually has the power to draw you closer to one another. Because God's commands are for us and are meant to lead to our growth, obedience to him always bears good fruit in our lives.

This does not mean, however, that the path in front of you will be easy. Following Christ happens when we deny ourselves and put to death what is sinful in our lives. But what better way is there to cultivate trust, respect, spiritual maturity, and godly character than to follow the counsel of the One who designed relationships and knows the best way for us to have satisfying relationships?

Growing in a healthy and godly relationship with your partner means that you grow in wisdom regarding God's design for pre-marriage relationships, as well as marriage itself. As you step out and away from living together, you'll find that you have fresh mental and emotional space to discover areas you may need to grow in. Communicating, resolving conflicts, serving, healing from past pain and relational turmoil, and dealing with the impact of sexual sin are all areas God has wisdom and insight for. Make a commitment to be a student of God's ways and Word, and ask him to mature you and strengthen your understanding of biblical truth in these areas.

Get engaged and proceed toward marriage

If you have followed the above steps and you have the affirmation of mature Christians and wise people in your life, you may be ready to move toward marriage.[5] God delights to bring people together in a Christ-centered, love-filled marriage!

Remember, marriage *is* a gift for people to enjoy, yet it also brings glory and joy to our God as Christian marriage models and points to his grace, love, and eternal commitment to his people. You now have the opportunity to experience the blessing of marriage, with God's favor resting upon you. Yes, marriage takes work, but you already know that—any successful relationship needs selfless focus.

Now move toward a relationship founded on the promise that brings the security needed to develop the kind of love and that will honor our Lord.

Endnotes

1. "The Downside of Cohabitating Before Marriage," April 14, 2012. Meg Jay comments in her article on the growing popularity of cohabitation. http://www.nytimes.com/2012/04/15/opinion/sunday/the-downside-of-cohabiting-before-marriage.html.

2. "Truth or Tradition: Do Christians need to be married by a minister or can we just commit to each other privately in God's sight." No author listed. This

article elaborates on the wisdom of a public ceremony. http://www.truthortradition.com/articles/do-christians-need-to-be-married-by-a-minister-or-can-we-just-commit-to-each-other-privately-in-gods-sight.

3. Quoted from John Piper, sermon, "Marriage: God's Showcase of Covenant Keeping Grace," February 7, 2011. http://www.desiringgod.org/sermons/marriage-god-s-showcase-of-covenant-keeping-grace.

4. Greg Gilbert, *What Is the Gospel?* (Wheaton, IL: Crossway, 2010), 81.

5. Two resources for wisely thinking through proceeding toward marriage are William P. Smith, *Should We Get Married? How to Evaluate Your Relationship* (Greensboro, NC: New Growth Press, 2010) and David Powlison and John Yenchko, *Pre-Engagement: 5 Questions to Ask Yourselves* (Resources for Changing Lives) (Phillipsburg, NJ: P&R, 2000).